TWENTY-FOUR CHANGES TO IMMEDIATELY IMPROVE YOUR HAPPINESS

ALSO FROM REVIVAL TODAY

Financial Overflow

Dominion Over Sickness and Disease

Boldly I Come: Praying According to God's Word

Twenty Secrets for an Unbreakable Marriage

How to Dominate in a Wicked Nation

Seven Wrong Relationships

Everything a Man Should Be

Understanding the World in Light of Bible Prophecy

Are You Going Through a Crisis?

The 20 Laws that Govern the Financial Anointing

35 Questions for Those Who Hate the Prosperity Gospel

The Art of Spiritual Warfare

Help for Your Darkest Time

Seven Reasons Your Church Will Never Have Revival

How God Heals Without Doctors, Medicine, or Surgery

Who Told You That You're in a Season of Waiting

How to Prevail in Every Battle of Life

Decisions Determine Destiny

Twenty-Four Changes to Immediately Improve Your Happiness

Taking Your Place at the Top

The Path to Dominion: A 16-Week Devotional to Walk in God's Plan for Your Life

TWENTY-FOUR CHANGES TO IMMEDIATELY IMPROVE YOUR HAPPINESS

JONATHAN SHUTTLESWORTH

Without limiting the rights under copyright(s) reserved below, no part of this publication may be reproduced, stored in, or introduced into a retrieval system or transmitted in any form or by any means (electronic, mechanical, photocopying, recording, or otherwise) without the prior permission of the publisher and the copyright owner.

The content of this book is provided "AS IS." The publisher and the author make no guarantees or warranties as to the accuracy, adequacy, or completeness of or results to be obtained from using the content of this book, including any information that can be accessed through hyperlinks or otherwise, and expressly disclaim any warranty expressed or implied, including but not limited to implied warranties of merchantability or fitness for a particular purpose. This limitation of liability shall apply to any claim or cause whatsoever, whether such claim or cause arises in contract, tort, or otherwise. In short, you, the reader, are responsible for your choices and the results they bring.

The scanning, uploading, and distributing of this book via the internet or any other means without the permission of the publisher and copyright owner is illegal and punishable by law. Please purchase only authorized copies, and do not participate in or encourage piracy of copyrighted materials. Your support of the author's rights is appreciated.

Scripture quotations marked (NLT) are taken from the Holy Bible, New Living Translation, copyright © 1996, 2004, 2015 by Tyndale House Foundation. Used by permission of Tyndale House Publishers, Inc., Carol Stream, Illinois 60188. All rights reserved.

Scripture quotations without attribution are from the King James Version of the Bible, which is in the public domain.

Scripture quotations marked (NKJV) are taken from the New King James Version®. Copyright © 1982 by Thomas Nelson. Used by permission. All rights reserved.

Copyright © 2025 by Revival Today. All rights reserved.

Released: December 2025
ISBN: 978-1-64457-780-6 (pb)

Rise UP Publications
www.riseUPpublications.com

From today forward, may all your wildest dreams come true. May you never know another day of sorrow all the days of your life.

— JONATHAN SHUTTLESWORTH

CONTENTS

Preface   9
Introduction   11

Change 1   17
Adjust Your Morning Routine

Change 2   19
Change the Company You Keep

Change 3   23
Immediately Remove Anyone Who Steals Your Joy or Causes Problems

Change 4   25
Fire Anyone Who Creates More Work for You

Change 5   27
Do Something That Makes You Happy Every Day

Change 6   31
Change Your Phone Number

Change 7   33
Develop a Gatekeeping System

Change 8   35
Find the Best Food Wherever You Are

Change 9   39
Give Yourself a Light at the End of the Tunnel

Change 10   41
Visit the Same Vacation Spot Every Time

Change 11   43
Learn to Not Care

Change 12   51
Stop Magnifying the Minute Faults of Those Close to You

Change 13   53
Send Someone a Gift Today and Every Week

Change 14   59
Never Leave Your Chariot to Chase a Fool

Change 15   63
Lower Your Goals

Change 16   65
Turn Your Vehicle into a Place You Enjoy

Change 17   67
Learn to Change Your Atmosphere

Change 18   73
Remove the Rebellious Immediately

Change 19   77
Remove Liars Immediately

Change 20   83
Find Someone or Something That Makes You Laugh and Listen or Watch It Every Day

Change 21   85
Keep Painful Memories in a Place You Can Access When You're Ready

Change 22   89
Find a Way to Do What You Love Most for a Living

Change 23   95
Do What You Do Your Way

Change 24   101
Stop Sinning

Afterword   103
Jonathan and Adalis Shuttlesworth   107

PREFACE

Few things are more maligned in Christianity than happiness. Many Christians will point out the differences between happiness and joy as if seeking happiness is diametrically opposed to having joy. It's true, visiting locations that make you happy won't necessarily bring you joy. Happiness is temporary, but what's wrong with temporary happiness? If I were to take a five-day vacation to enjoy time with my family, I would experience happiness from breaking away from the norm to get away with my family, but I wouldn't base my salvation on how good taking the trip made me feel. This could be why so many Christians are unhappy—all we ever seem to hear in church is negativity toward happiness.

An oppressed, depressed mind doesn't think clearly. Few inventions come from people in mental institutions. Your mind must be in a certain state to produce effectively. That's why the Devil fights against your happiness—and why God is not opposed to it.

PREFACE

One thing to note in the Gospels—Matthew, Mark, Luke, and John—is that Jesus made people happy. When a sad woman approached Jesus with news her son had died, Jesus raised her son from the dead, and the woman was filled with happiness. Jesus didn't go around making happy people sad. He made sad people very happy. He healed the blind, and as a result, they said, *"I once was blind, but now I see!"*

Growing up, I had what some Christians might call a disease: I was happy all the time. I was constantly told to stop laughing. When I was in school, they tried to paddle it out of me as best they could, but it was no use. I might be one of the most qualified people to write a book on happiness because I've been happy my whole life.

I've never fit in well with most Christians because not only are they often unhappy, but they also seem to enjoy being that way. Many Christians think there's something spiritual about being stern. When you instruct a congregation to pray, most don't pray—they just look mean.

The main reason why *Check the News* has grown such a large audience is because my interpretation of the news never came from a depressed, conservative perspective. I'm probably one of the few happy conservatives on television and one of the few happy Christians.

I don't know why Christians devalue happiness and actively speak against it. Yes, we do need joy, but we can have both. Most of the people who claim Christians should have joy rather than happiness don't have either. This book will reveal changes you can make to experience both.

INTRODUCTION

Before we dive into the changes necessary to improve your happiness, I want to provide you with seven reasons why you should prioritize it.

1. GOD DID NOT CREATE THIS LIFE TO BE ENDURED; HE CREATED IT TO BE ENJOYED

The Bible says, *"Charge them that are rich in this world, that they be not highminded, nor trust in uncertain riches, but in the living God, who giveth us richly all things to enjoy"* (1 Timothy 6:17). He doesn't just give us the things we need, He gives us richly all things to enjoy.

"I have come that they may have life, and that they may have it more abundantly" (John 10:10 **NKJV**). God desires for you to have an abundant, enjoyable, and fulfilling life. He didn't create the world for the Devil's children to enjoy. He created it for believers to enjoy.

INTRODUCTION

> Then the people of Israel set out from Mount Hor, taking the road to the Red Sea to go around the land of Edom. But the people grew impatient with the long journey, and they began to speak against God and Moses. "Why have you brought us out of Egypt to die here in the wilderness?" they complained. "There is nothing to eat here and nothing to drink. And we hate this horrible manna!" So the Lord sent poisonous snakes among the people, and many were bitten and died.
>
> — NUMBERS 21:4-6 (NLT)

An unhappy person *irritates* God. Your unhappiness will lead you to complain. Joy and praise coincide in the same way unhappiness and complaining go hand in hand.

2. UNHAPPY PEOPLE REPEL GOD—AND EVERYONE ELSE

This is not meant to be a shot at people who are going through a problem and need help. This is geared toward *complainers*. God parted the Red Sea, fed the Israelites manna from Heaven for free, and they *still* complained. So, God sent vipers to bite them. God doesn't send snakes after us in the New Testament, but if He did, most Christians would be dead. Jesus took our punishment for us.

The consequences may have changed, but God's nature never changes. God *despises* complainers. You could make the argument God despises the unhappy because unhappy people complain. If you think there's something spiritual about being unhappy, think again. I don't know why Christians place such a low premium on happiness because the Bible instructs us to *"Rejoice in the Lord always"* (Philippians 4:4). Unhappiness is a violation of what God commanded.

3. YOU MUST BUILD YOUR HAPPINESS BECAUSE SORROW BUILDS ITSELF

You don't have to make any effort to experience sorrow; it comes freely if you aren't determined to build your happiness. Something will fill your life—either happiness or sorrow. You don't *fall* into happiness—you *build* it. Happiness requires effort. If you don't make the effort to create and cultivate happiness, sorrow will build itself.

4. A HAPPY YOU IS THE BEST YOU

Joel Osteen is probably the most-watched preacher in the world. If he's not the most-watched worldwide, he's certainly the most-watched in America and is among the top globally. Christians criticize Joel Osteen nonstop: "He just smiles. He doesn't even really say anything." That proves the value of happiness. For many people, Joel Osteen is the only happy person they encounter all day. Their children are miserable. Their spouse is miserable. Their boss is miserable. Their coworkers are miserable. "But he opens with a joke," people grumble. And look how far it has brought him. There's value in making people happy. A happy you is the best you.

5. A HAPPY YOU IS THE MOST PRODUCTIVE YOU

God, your Creator, knows how you perform best and how you can get the most out of life. Only a happy you can influence people positively for Christ. No one wants to know the God of a depressed person.

INTRODUCTION

People aren't interested in hearing about the hope you have if you look like you'd fling yourself off a five-story building at any moment.

6. UNHAPPINESS ATTRACTS OPPRESSION

Unhappiness repels everything except the Devil. It attracts the Devil. Complaining and murmuring invite demonic activity into your life. Have you ever noticed that you never feel good when you talk about negative things? You never feel better discussing how much you dislike your church or your boss. So, don't dwell on bad things. Instead, speak about good things. *"Bless the Lord, O my soul, and forget not all His benefits"* (Psalm 103:2). Speak of His benefits. Speak of good things. God isn't the One who benefits when we rejoice and feel happy. He's already happy. He told us to rejoice because it helps *us*.

7. HAPPINESS ATTRACTS FAVOR

Most employers would rather hire someone who's enjoyable to be around over a candidate who may do a better job but isn't as likable. That's been my secret in nearly every job I've worked: I made the boss laugh. I made my ice hockey coach laugh, and as a result, he made me captain even though I was the worst player by far. He'd call me into his office and say, "Make me laugh."

When I went to a Christian school, I was punished for laughing. When I attended public school, my eighth-grade English teacher, Mr. Hayes, would ask me to stay after class to make him laugh, and then write me a late slip for my next class. He thought I was hilarious. The last I heard, he was working for Border Patrol at the Maine-Canada border. When my sister, Jessica, passed through that crossing, he was the border patrol agent. He recognized the last name and asked her, "Shuttlesworth? How's your brother, Jonathan, doing?" He started smiling, just thinking about me. Imagine that. You'll do well in life if people start laughing at the mention of your name.

Several of my friends smile from ear to ear after mentioning my name. They can't help but grin before they even begin the story they're preparing to tell the congregation about me. I've met people like that—anytime you see them, they leave you smiling. I try to leave people laughing before hanging up the phone, like I'm ending a radio interview. I make it a point to end the conversation on a high note.

Happiness attracts favor. Notice how people feel when they leave your presence. Do they think, 'What can I do to have that person around more?' Or are they thinking, 'What can I do to make sure that person is never around again?' Happiness attracts favor because when you're so happy that your joy overflows to others, they'll be intentional about having you around more often. Happiness is important. It's not an accident—it's something you cultivate.

You're about to discover twenty-four changes that you can make to immediately improve your happiness today. Let's dig in!

CHANGE 1

ADJUST YOUR MORNING ROUTINE

What you smell and drink in the morning matters greatly and contributes to your overall happiness. If the twenty-four-year-old me read this, he'd probably try to beat me up, but I'll write it anyway: buy candles. I never thought the day would come when I'd buy a candle for my house, but it matters. Thank God you can control the scent of your home because sandalwood smells better than a wet dog. There are little things you can put in your house that make a big difference.

What do you have in your refrigerator or cupboard that makes you happy—something that makes you look forward to getting up when the alarm goes off? I'm not Oprah Winfrey, so I'm not going to give you a list of recommendations, but I researched the best coffee I could buy, and Intelligentsia Coffee was at the top of every list. You might have a different opinion, and I'm not saying this *is* the best, but three different sources placed it in their top five, so I ordered it. When it arrived, I anticipated making it the next morning, and when my alarm went off, I immediately had something to look forward to instead of just thinking, 'Oh, it's time to get up.'

My mother sent me a Tea Forte box set, and it's the best tea I've ever had. Daniel and Karen Bracken sent me honey from their honey farm in Wasilla, Alaska, and it's the best honey I've ever had. Put them together, and you're in for an enjoyable morning cup of tea. These aren't expensive things, but they add happiness to my morning. Have something enjoyable planned every morning, even if it's as simple as your coffee or tea.

I'll add another idea for your morning routine. Even though my wife and I had been married for eighteen years, we were still using the same towels from when we were first married. They were ratty, and using them made me unhappy. So, I ordered Forbes List's top-rated towels. They were more expensive than regular towels, but they weren't an insane amount. Some things are worth paying for, especially if you use them every day. Towels, I'm hoping, are something you use daily.

My wife was very surprised to discover I ordered new towels. She never thought I'd buy something like that for the house. They're plush, and we all love them—my daughter especially. Instead of a worn-out, hole-ridden towel waiting for me, I now have the plushest towel known to man, free from bleach stains, and it makes me happy. I'm sure someone will wonder, 'Why is he writing about towels when souls are going to hell?' The truth is that I can do both—I can have a good towel and still pursue souls. Towels aren't more important than souls, but this isn't a deep doctrinal masterpiece. It's just something practical about happiness because little changes can make a big difference.

CHANGE 2

CHANGE THE COMPANY YOU KEEP

This change can be broken down into two parts because who you associate with includes both removing people and adding others. Let's begin with who you should keep at arm's length distance.

1. DISTANCE YOURSELF FROM PEOPLE WHO MAKE YOU UNHAPPY—AVOID THEM AT ALL COSTS.

If you have to meet with someone you don't enjoy being around, meet at a coffee shop. (Just because I've met you at a coffee shop doesn't mean I don't like you.) If you can't get away with meeting at a café, meet at a restaurant, but keep in mind it's a longer time commitment. If you take a meeting at a coffee shop, you can keep it to twelve minutes and be on your way. If you're unsure how a meeting will go, choose a café, and don't feel bad about leaving. When you're ready, tell the person you enjoyed the conversation, stand up, and go. If they try to continue the conversation, have them walk with you as you head to your car. If there's one thing I'm a master at, it's knowing how to leave.

Never meet with someone in their home if they're not someone who brings you joy or if you don't know them well. When you meet at someone's house, there's no set end time. Plus there's always a possibility you could end up dead via blunt object or boredom. Meet in a public place instead. My heart goes out to pastors who haven't learned this lesson and still meet with people in their homes.

The difference between a fifteen-minute meeting and a four-hour meeting is three hours and forty-five minutes. That's a considerable amount of time you could have spent with your family. I haven't tried this yet, but I'm not against meeting on the curb, rolling down the window, and driving off when we've finished our business.

Another thing I'd advise against is getting in the car with people—always drive yourself. Don't pick people up or have them pick you up. Drive so you can leave when you need to.

Here's a practical example of how you can apply this point. A woman I know was getting ready to celebrate her birthday. She shares a birthday with her young son and would typically invite extended family over to celebrate because she assumed it was the proper thing to do, but it always stressed her out. She'd spend hours cleaning the house and mentally preparing herself to host people she didn't particularly enjoy being around. One year, she simply decided not to have people over on her birthday. It was an epiphany: she could celebrate her birthday without extended family, and just like that, she looked forward to her birthday again. Her husband brought her son to see family and open presents while she enjoyed her day. No stress. No speed-tongues. Just peace.

A very powerful minister told me something that changed my life. When I was in my early twenties, I asked him one thing he would change if he could go back in time and be my age. I expected him to say something like read the Bible more often or pray and fast every month, but I was way off. He told me he would have made a point to always do whatever made things easiest for him. It was the complete opposite of everything I was taught in Bible college. I was taught to allow people to run you to death as if being a doormat was at the heart of service.

Noticing the crease in my brow, he gave me examples of what he meant by 'easiest for him.' He said, "When I would drive through the night to get to church to preach on Sunday morning, it left me exhausted after service. The pastor would always invite me out to lunch, and I usually said yes. I should have declined, driven back to my hotel to sleep, and met up with the pastor later that evening. If I could go back in time, I wouldn't allow anyone to make me feel like I *had* to do anything," he offered.

This came from a power minister of a very influential ministry. After he explained it to me, I took it as permission to do the same. Then I saw the same principle in the Bible. In John 7, the disciples wanted Jesus to go with them to the Festival of Tabernacle, but He declined and went alone. When Mary and Martha sent a messenger to insist Jesus come to heal Lazarus, He didn't rush to get there. He withdrew to the wilderness instead. Lazarus was dying a very short distance away from Jesus' location. Jesus never rushed, and He never allowed anyone to force Him into doing anything.

People will try to make you feel it's not Christ-like to avoid the people and things you don't enjoy, but that's how Jesus operated on Earth.

2. SPEND TIME WITH PEOPLE WHO MAKE YOU HAPPY

Surround yourself with people who make you happy. There should be something about them that you enjoy. Our ministry is staffed with high-energy people, and I'll keep it that way for the rest of my life. It's by design that I enjoy being around every single person employed by our ministry. If I didn't, they wouldn't be here. Many people in ministry dread going into their office because it's filled with people who bring them down. Most church offices feel like the waiting room at Sloan Kettering Cancer Center. Who you surround yourself with matters—spend time with people who make you happy. If you don't own your own business, you may not have control over your coworkers, but you can control who you're around when you're off the clock.

I have a friend in the ministry who I don't get to see very often. When I finally did cross paths with him, I invited him to come grab something to eat with me. He didn't even respond to my question. He just looked over at his wife, she shook her head "yes", and off we went. Later, I joked and asked him if he'd like me to ask his wife directly next time or better yet, bring a permission slip for her to sign. I don't understand why people marry someone who constantly yells and corrects them. You have control over who you're friends with and who you marry.

CHANGE 3

IMMEDIATELY REMOVE ANYONE WHO STEALS YOUR JOY OR CAUSES PROBLEMS

This applies to those who own a business: Get rid of anyone who causes problems or steals your joy. I wouldn't keep anyone in my environment if I had to struggle to stay happy around them. Anyone who works for me is welcome to bring things up if needed, but in all my years in ministry, not one person has approached me to talk about what's going wrong. They're not wired that way. They're on the phone helping others right now. They're positive people who know how to handle their own troubles. They're welcome to talk to me, but it wouldn't be a daily thing.

My grandfather, who pastored for sixty-two years, used to say, "Problems in life are free. There's no reason to put them on the payroll." Don't employ problems. I hear some people talk about their staff, and my only thought is, 'Why do you pay them?' You've put them on salary to ensure they never leave your life? Sounds like the problem is with you. Fire people. Find a creative way to move them on. I don't mean anything extreme, like burying the body—you don't have to fire them harshly, just do what's necessary to follow this principle.

CHANGE 4

FIRE ANYONE WHO CREATES MORE WORK FOR YOU

You hire people to take things *off* your plate, not to put things *on* it. Everyone hired at this ministry was brought on so we could minister to more people, not to add people to my immediate environment who also need ministering. Everyone on our staff is a co-laborer.

I was on a trip with a pastor who received a call because his staff couldn't find the keys to unlock the church for service that night. He asked his employee if he had asked another staff member, and they had never thought to do so before calling the senior pastor while he was hundreds of miles away. This happened a while ago when I was more outspoken. When the pastor hung up the phone, I told him flat out, "If I were you, I'd fire that person."

If you don't own your own business or run your own ministry, one way to get promoted is to be like Joseph in Genesis. The Bible says the prison warden's only decision was what to eat because Joseph took care of everything else.

Rom, our production manager, has never called to ask me if I can help him troubleshoot why the internet is down. He just handles it. I'm sure he addresses plenty of technical issues, but I never hear about them. Rom never calls me about problems. I asked him to create our 24-hour broadcast network on the app because I knew the days of Facebook and YouTube allowing ministries to preach freely were numbered. The next time I heard about it was when it was done. Rom didn't mention the app again until it was about to launch. "Remember the app you asked us to build? It took six months, but it'll be ready in three weeks. Here's the beta version."

Hire people who take work *off* your plate, not people who check in with you for every decision. If employees call you about every little thing, maybe you've trained them to do so. When you control everything, they'll feel like they have to call you for everything.

When the insurance company for the ministry threatened to drop us, I never heard about it until after it was over. Patrick handled it. I can't imagine him ever asking me what to do about insurance. How the heck should I know? That's Patrick's job, and he does it well. Because he does it well, it enables me to do the things that make me happy, which is studying the Word and preaching.

Hire people who free you up to have vision, enjoy your work, and focus on what you love to do.

CHANGE 5

DO SOMETHING THAT MAKES YOU HAPPY EVERY DAY

Why do people feel guilty for doing something that makes them happy? I'm over forty years old, and I still play video games without a hint of guilt. It's not heroin. It's not a sin to play video games. I think people have been programmed to believe that if something brings you pleasure, it must be wrong. If something is not listed in the Bible as a sin, there's no reason to feel bad about enjoying it. If you find pleasure in something the Bible calls a sin, you shouldn't do it at all—not even occasionally.

Whatever makes you happy that isn't sinful or illegal, do it every day that you possibly can. I don't golf, but if I did, I'd go to the driving range every day if it put me in a good mood. I know CEOs who use their lunch hour to golf, go to the gun range, or hunt.

I enjoy playing *Modern Warfare Warzone* online with select friends and family. We laugh hard—very hard. It makes me happy, and I clear time for it daily when I'm home, but I don't do it when I'm on the road preaching. I can spend time with God and also enjoy my day.

Do you think video games will replace God in my life? I'm not going to suddenly wake up one day and insist that Adalis take Camila to church without me while I stay home and worship my Xbox. The two activities fulfill different roles. Coffee is also important to me, but it will never replace God in my life. There's no competition, but there's also no need to choose.

I remember when my nephew was getting married, and my wife needed a dress for the occasion. She asked me if I was okay with her going shopping for the rest of the evening. I handed her all the money I had on me, which was a good amount, and told her to buy all the dresses she wanted for as long as she wanted and to have fun. Why give your spouse a hard time about something they enjoy? Would you rather drive them to a bar? Don't marry someone who resents what makes you happy, and don't make your spouse feel bad about what they love to do.

Here's a novel idea for those who aren't married: marry someone you enjoy being with. I married Adalis because she made me happy every time I saw her. She made me happy to be with her. She was funny. I don't understand why some men look to marry a mother figure or a drill sergeant. A man's wife asked me to stop talking about how much I play video games because her husband played all the time, and it bothered her. I know her husband. He's a good guy who works hard, provides for his family, and only plays video games for an hour or two each day. I've counseled women whose husbands have serious issues with substance abuse, violence, or affairs. This woman's husband didn't have a substance abuse problem or a mistress, he simply wanted to play video games at home for an hour each day. He wasn't running guns to Panama. If she continues to give him a hard time, I wouldn't be surprised if he ended up with a mistress or a drinking problem. Why make your husband miserable in his own home? It will lead to more serious issues.

To be clear, my suggestion is to find something that makes you happy and isn't illegal or sinful and do it every day. I'm not implying you should do it *all day*, every day. You shouldn't do what makes you happy and ignore your wife and children to do it. This advice is directed at reasonable, intelligent people. If you love golf, I suggest going to the driving range every day, not playing thirty-six holes a day, and coming home at 10 p.m. Do what makes you happy, and don't feel guilty. This change requires reciprocity. If you allow your spouse to enjoy what they love without guilt, they're likely to do the same for you.

Adalis embodies this principle. When we were first married, Adalis and I used to spend time playing video games together, and she'd often play longer than I did. One year, rather than get upset that I played Fantasy Football, she joined me. She drafted Tom Brady and Randy Moss the year they connected for twenty-two touchdowns. She went undefeated, won the championship, and decided not to play anymore because it was *"too easy."* Those were some of the best days of our marriage. Marriage has phases. The first few years without kids are special. You and your spouse get to spend every evening together—just the two of you. Unlike dating, you don't have to say goodbye—you just get to spend uninterrupted time together.

Here's another thought: marry someone who enjoys the same things you enjoy. If you love playing video games, don't marry someone who hates that you play. If you like to golf, don't marry a woman who hates that you golf. Maybe marry a golfer. Don't set your life up to be frustrated. If you're not married, choose someone who shares your interests. If you love hunting, marry a hunter. If you love playing video games, marry a gamer. If you're already married, then it's too late. So, identify something that makes you happy, and if it's not illegal and it's not a sin, do it every day, and don't feel bad about it.

CHANGE 6

CHANGE YOUR PHONE NUMBER

There's a famous preacher who used to change his phone number every thirty days. Whenever someone asked him for his phone number, he'd agree without hesitation because it was only a matter of time before you no longer had it. If too many people have your phone number, you might benefit from changing it. As a pastor, your church will not reach a certain level of growth if everyone in the congregation has your number. Your phone becomes a tool the Devil uses to distract you from your purpose. You can't let others dictate your schedule—you need control over your time. If everyone can call you whenever they want, you have a problem.

Once you change your number, use your caller ID judiciously. You don't have to answer every call, nor should you. I have friends with unlisted numbers who struggle to reach me. When they finally catch up with me, they mention how they've been trying to get ahold of me. We eventually identified the problem when I discovered they were calling from a private number. "You'll never reach me that way," I tell them. I'm not gambling every time I answer the phone.

There was a time when TMZ tried everything to contact me. They even called my mother at her house. Local reporters tried reaching me, too. I'm not answering the phone blindly, and I'm certainly not answering the door blindly.

Don't be a slave to your phone. Some people think it's a constitutional duty to answer every call, regardless of who's calling. Not me. I take extreme measures to avoid talking to people who don't make me happy. I once had a lady's number marked in my phone as "depressed woman, do not answer." I don't know how she got my number. I had another person saved as "crazy woman, do not answer." She would call for help, but I always felt like I needed a nap after getting off the phone with her—she'd drain the life out of me. Use your caller ID.

Don't give people the power to snap you out of a good mood, or allow the Devil to use someone to disrupt or dictate your day with an unexpected call. Set a course and stay on it. Talk to people when you're ready, not when they decide to bring their problems to you. Don't let someone else's issues consume two hours of your time, even if they're family.

CHANGE 7

DEVELOP A GATEKEEPING SYSTEM

Not everyone should have access to you at their leisure. Last year, a person came up to me at a church and apologized for sending me a negative letter. They went on and on about how they were going through a rough time and not serving the Lord as they should have and said things in that letter they didn't mean. I told them there was no need to apologize because I had never received the letter. Negative letters never make their way to me. How am I supposed to stay happy by reading letters from people who think I'm the Devil? Reading those would affect anyone.

Develop a gatekeeping system. Place someone in charge of filtering your calls and emails so that people can't just place something in front of your eyes anytime they want. If the Devil wants to discourage me, he has to go through at least two people before he reaches me. Miracles make it to my eyes. Testimonies make it to my eyes, but messages from people itching to tell me they think I'm one of the false prophets preceding the return of Christ or Satan himself—I don't see any of that. This helps keep me happy.

CHANGE 8

FIND THE BEST FOOD WHEREVER YOU ARE

Enjoying food is a pleasure God has given us. It's not a necessary evil, and King Solomon, the wisest man on Earth, emphasized this with his writing in Ecclesiastes.

> So I decided there is nothing better than to enjoy food and drink and to find satisfaction in work. Then I realized that these pleasures are from the hand of God.
>
> — ECCLESIASTES 2:24 (NLT)

I've had people apologize to me for eating while I was on a fast. I'm never offended when people talk about food, especially when I'm fasting. I prefer you talk about food in great detail. Let me live vicariously as you describe every ingredient of your meal. My dad was like that too. He used to cook for our family while he was on a fast. The absence of eating isn't the hardest part of fasting. It's the lack of time spent sitting and talking with your family and other people over food. Fasting causes you to realize how much of life centers around food.

Find the best food in your area because the best food isn't always the most expensive. Adalis found a new taco place nearby and claims it's as good as the tacos we had on the Mexican border during the crusades in California and Texas. I'm looking forward to trying it!

I know traveling ministers who only talk about how difficult it is to travel, because they don't know how to live on the road. The only way they can fathom traveling to preach long-term is if they could just appear at the church with a mic in hand. They hate traveling, they hate eating on the road, they hate staying in hotels, they hate everything that goes along with their assignment, but they don't have to live that way—it's a choice. If I ate at TGI Fridays and Applebee's every night, I'd hate traveling too. I decided to do everything possible to enjoy traveling.

In America, it's rare to travel to a place without at least one excellent restaurant, but when I come across a place without a great restaurant, I just fast that week. I once preached in St. Mary's, West Virginia, where the only option was Wendy's. Eating at Wendy's all week would result in me meeting Jesus sooner than planned! When your only food options are Wendy's or pre-wrapped gas station sandwiches, it's an easy call to fast, but when I travel to Houston, Texas, I don't fast—I know the best places to eat. Name a city I've been to, and I can tell you where to eat. I usually don't allow the pastor to choose the restaurant. I've found that most pastors don't know where to eat, even in their own city. I pay for the meal, and I choose the restaurant. I can't count how many times a pastor has told me they discovered more great restaurants in one week of eating with me than they have in two years in their city. I don't default to Applebee's. Use the technology available to you. I use Yelp to find the best places to eat. It's a great resource to find places you will enjoy.

There's a great restaurant not far from our church in Pittsburgh. The owner and sole cook is a woman who immigrated from South Korea. She's like a South Korean grandma. She takes your order, then heads to the kitchen to cook your meal. Everyone says it's the best South Korean food they've ever had. It's not expensive, but it's better than Capital Grille, no question. If we were in Philadelphia, I would take you to a cheesesteak spot and you'd eat better than you would at Ruth's Chris Steak House for eight bucks.

It's not about money. Food is a major part of life. I follow accounts on social media just to stay up to date on great places to eat. In almost every place I visit to preach, there's a restaurant I look forward to eating or trying for the first time. It adds enjoyment to my travel schedule. You won't do something you're sick of for long. The Lord called me to travel and preach, which means I need to find ways to do it that make me happy. I refuse to simply endure my assignment. There are already enough unavoidable things in life that require endurance, but I refuse to endure through self-inflicted problems.

Goldbelly is an app available on your phone that features the best foods in America. The choices range from Philadelphia cheesesteaks, cold subs from White House Subs in Atlantic City, and steaks from Peter Luger's (the steak Johnny Carson called the best meal he'd ever had.) You can order the best barbecue from the Midwest, key lime pie from the original location it was created in the Florida Keys, you name it. Famous bakeries, sandwich shops, and chicken places—they're all on Goldbelly, and you can have it shipped to your door. It's not cheap, but if you do it once a month, you'll have something to look forward to every month. If you can't afford to order every month, do it once every three months. I'd rather have one good meal than twenty lousy ones. If you like Applebee's, knock yourself out. If you prefer eating food with nine times the suggested sodium content that makes you thirsty for a week, go ahead—I'm not here to judge.

Magalis, our ministry's head administrator, used to order something from Goldbelly for the staff every month. When you have something special waiting at the office, you look forward to going to work. The Bible says there's nothing better than eating, drinking, and finding pleasure in your work. All of this is a gift from God. It's a blessing to enjoy food. That's why, when we pray over a meal, we ask God to nourish it to our bodies as we thank Him for it. We acknowledge that it's a gift from God to sit down, enjoy our food, and talk with our loved ones over a meal. When it comes to temporal things, there's nothing better than enjoying good food, so you might as well enjoy it.

CHANGE 9

GIVE YOURSELF A LIGHT AT THE END OF THE TUNNEL

In 2020, I went through stretches of time where I did the most work I had ever done in my life. I hosted a two-hour broadcast in the early afternoon, another four hours with Pastor Rodney, and then *Check the News* for an hour and a half at night. I'd leave home at 12:30 p.m. and get back around 2:00 a.m. and was on air almost the entire time. When I wasn't on air, I was preparing for the next show. I kept that schedule for three months straight, but by the end of May, I had a trip planned with Adalis and Camila. After that stretch of extreme productivity, I ended up with more meetings scheduled than I ever had before, plus three churches and a Bible school. I still operate the same way, but I always plan time away with my family.

Give yourself a light at the end of the tunnel. Work as hard as you can on your God-given assignment. Pursue and develop your dream, but make sure you have something to look forward to. If you can't afford a vacation in another state, find a spot ninety minutes from home where you can drive with your spouse and kids. If you're single, find a place you enjoy going alone—ideally somewhere with a low chance of being murdered. (I've noticed on *Forensic Files* that state parks aren't always the best choice for solo trips!)

Plan a trip, even if it's not far or exotic. Find a lake, a sporting event, or something similar. The idea is to work hard but have a payoff. Plan incremental getaways so that you always have that light at the end of the tunnel. I don't mean plan a trip that you'll take two years from now—I mean something every three or four months.

CHANGE 10

VISIT THE SAME VACATION SPOT EVERY TIME

This is more of a tip than a change you can make. Rodney Howard-Browne gave me this advice, and I'm glad I listened. Now I'm passing it on to you. As soon as you arrive at a familiar resort, campground, or favorite spot, all the memories from previous visits come flooding back. It does something to you mentally—within the first hour, you feel like you've been there for a month. You already know where to eat, and there's no wasted time or meals. It didn't take long for what Pastor Rodney described to start happening when we traveled.

Find a place you can fall in love with, and make it a yearly tradition. I found my spot in Arizona, and I'm not looking anywhere else. I know where to eat, where to drive, and where to go. The moment I land, I feel like I've been living there for years. There's no need to settle in or adjust, and there's no awkward first day of not knowing where to park or where things are located. It's like returning to a home you've lived in for a long time.

Try it. Do your research and find your spot. I don't know anyone from Pennsylvania who vacations in Arizona—most people like Myrtle Beach or Hilton Head. Every region has popular vacation spots. If you love your local attractions, choose one, but also consider exploring. Google Maps is a great place to start. Sometimes, the planning itself is as enjoyable as the trip. I alternate between a few places: I love Page, Arizona, up by the Utah border. I spend time in Sedona, and I really enjoy Scottsdale.

CHANGE 11

LEARN TO NOT CARE

DON'T TIE ASPECTS OF YOUR HAPPINESS TO SOMEONE ELSE'S DECISIONS, FAULTS, OR LIFE

If this is contrary to what you've heard from every other minister your whole life, I apologize but learn to *not care*. Don't allow any part of your happiness to be tied to other people's decisions or lives. If you wish your mother would stop drinking, pray about your mother's alcoholism. Pray about your sister's anger problem, but don't tie your happiness to it. What I mean by "don't care," is to commit it to the Lord in prayer. Kenneth Hagin said, "And then don't touch it in your thought life." Some people, and Christians especially, tie their emotions to other people's problems under the guise of having a burden or praying for someone. If you've prayed about it, you should no longer be sad about it—that's unscriptural. *"Believing that you have received, you shall have whatsoever things you ask"* (Mark 11:24). When you truly believe, you don't allow your happiness to depend on others' choices.

If your friend has been sick for a long time and you've told her about my teaching on healing, invited her to a virtual healing meeting, and given her T.L. Osborne's book, but she hasn't read it, then you've done all you can. When Jesus told the rich young ruler to follow Him, the man refused and walked away. The Bible says Jesus watched him go (Matthew 19:16-26). Don't tie your happiness to someone else's life, decisions, or problems.

I decided a long time ago not to care more about someone's life than they do themselves. I'll help, but if you're not interested, I won't push. People are who they are. Don't focus on the happiness of people who are intent on being unhappy. Some people don't want a cure—they love being miserable. Let them be miserable. If they want to be unhappy, they're welcome to be unhappy, but you can't care more about their lives than they do.

Don't tie any aspect of your happiness to someone else's decisions, faults, or life. Once you reach this place, you've entered a level of happiness where *you're* in charge. Don't let anyone else decide your happiness. If your mother is Baptist and won't come to your church, accept it. If she's a Baptist and doesn't care about the Holy Ghost or healing or speaking in tongues, what are you going to do about it? If God can't persuade her, why are you trying? Enjoy people for who they are, not who you wish they'd be.

We all have people close to us who don't value what we do. Maybe you wish your father valued what you do for work. If he doesn't, you need to move on. Maybe your mother didn't send anything for your birthday. Move on. *Don't* care. It could be that your mother forgets things, or maybe she's selfish. Now that you've established that fact, stop letting it bother you—especially things that happened decades ago. Let it go. Maybe your dad never went to your baseball games. Are you going to forgive him, or are you going to carry that to Hell with you? Learn to not care.

Learn to live for *God's* approval. Find your fulfillment in what God thinks about you. There are people close to me who couldn't care less about what I do in ministry. When I hear from them, it's like they're reading their partners letter to me—they don't ask, and they don't know where I'm preaching. You can tell they don't care. I accept it. Probably over half the people reading this have a father who doesn't care about you, what you do, or what you're up against. Many men are wired that way. If your dad didn't care at fifty, he's likely not going to start now. Stop caring about it. People have flaws. They don't know how to celebrate anyone's success, or they aren't interested in anyone except themselves—just deal with it.

Yes, it does hurt if your mother doesn't know or care about what you do. She might still think you work at your old job or not even know you changed jobs three years ago. Instead of focusing on that, leave it to God. Celebrate the fact that she got you out of the house alive and didn't overdose on heroin when you were a toddler, which is more than many people can say. Stop wishing for people to take roles in your life that they're not going to fill. We'd all love for our dads to be our biggest cheerleaders, but don't let that turn you into a miserable person. Move on. Don't try to make someone fill a role they're not suited for.

If everyone grew up with my mother, we'd all be in Heaven by now. The rapture would have already happened because there wouldn't be anyone left unsaved. She's my biggest cheerleader—she calls or texts me after every message to say, "That was the best I've ever heard you preach," or "Tonight was the best *Check the News* you've ever done." I tell her, "Mom, you said that last night," but she replies, "No, but tonight was even better." That's just how she is. It would be nice if everyone had a mom like her, but my mom didn't even grow up with a mom like her. My grandmother didn't even look at my mom's report card.

It hurts to grow up with a father who doesn't give a crap about your life, but don't let it determine your happiness. If your mother missed your graduation or wedding and would probably find a way to miss your funeral, accept that flaw, realize she's selfish, and stop tying your happiness to her deliverance. God will send other people into your life. The Devil's goal is to make you so upset, sad, and unhappy that you never reach your destiny. Don't let it hinder you—God will place people in your life who will celebrate you if you keep your happiness.

Timothy's father isn't mentioned in the Bible, but God sent him a father in Paul. *"Anyone who gives up fathers or mothers for my sake and the gospel will receive now in this life mothers and fathers"* (Matthew 19:29). That's God's promise. He'll provide spiritual mothers and fathers who care about you and pray for you. Look at Paul's words to Timothy: *"Timothy, I pray for you night and day. I want you to make full proof of your ministry"* (2 Timothy 4:5). Paul knew Timothy, he prayed for him, and he cared about him. If someone doesn't take the role they should, God will send someone else.

Whatever you wish someone would do for you, do that for others. Sow what you don't have. Remember that principle. Do you think it's a coincidence that my grandmother didn't show any interest in my mother's report card or college graduation, and now my mother is the complete opposite? My mom decided that when she had kids, she would care about everything they did. She became the antithesis of her own mother's neglect. That's worth celebrating.

I've worked with people in ministry who had no place for the Holy Ghost. I was upset that they didn't take their ministry seriously, but it made me detest unspiritual ministry. It provoked me to pursue the Holy Spirit even more. What the Devil intends for harm, God uses for good.

Some of you had parents who didn't care about what you did and showed no interest, so your experience likely made you take extra interest in your child's life. You can go one of two ways: You can let it drag you down, or you can determine to move in the opposite direction. Maybe the Lord used that experience so you would have a disgust toward certain behaviors. It could be that the reason you're so unselfish is because your parents were extremely selfish. Maybe you place a high premium upon God and His Word because your parents didn't, and you see the difficulties it brought to their lives. You should be thankful for that. Honor them for getting you out of the house alive.

Don't try to turn people into who they aren't, and don't tie your happiness to whether or not someone changes. Tie it to what you can control. You need to be able to intercede for people without letting their issues affect your happiness. Whenever I finish praying for someone, I leave it with the Lord. Stressing about it won't make it happen any faster. The Devil wants to destroy them and have the burden of it destroy me, too. I'm not letting that happen. If you've struggled with this in the past, I hope you felt something lift just now.

Learn not to care. If your mother told you she's not coming to your wedding, send her a food from Goldbelly. When it's obvious the Devil wants you to cry, do the opposite. Send her a gift with a card that says, "Love you, Mom. Sorry you couldn't make it to the wedding. Thanks for getting me out of the house alive and not overdosing on heroin."

Don't tie your happiness to whether your kids forgive you. That's manipulation, even if it's true. Would you want God to bring up your faults every time you missed the mark? Wisdom doesn't automatically come with age. A person who's foolish at twenty-two may still be foolish at sixty-two. Your dad may never grow out of certain behaviors, and that's a reality you have to accept. You may have parents who've never told you they loved you. Don't base your happiness on whether they ever do. Some people are screwed up. Come to grips with it. Don't let what others do affect you—decide to be their opposite. Allow God to use their faults to take faults out of you.

God can use what the Devil meant for harm to rid you of those traits. Were your parents selfish? I bet you're unselfish. Did your parents discourage church attendance? I bet you encourage your kids to serve the Lord with all their hearts. Every battle you faced growing up, your kids will never have to fight because they have a happy mom or dad.

If you ever learned the details about your parents' childhoods, you might realize they've come a long way. Maybe they weren't there for you, but they didn't beat you, even though their parents beat them. They might see themselves as "parent of the year" because they've come a long way from where they started. Hearing about people's backgrounds often puts things in perspective. They may have a long way to go, but they've also come a long way. So love them as they are, flaws and all.

STOP FINDING YOUR HAPPINESS IN OTHER PEOPLE'S APPROVAL

Maybe your mom doesn't approve of your job. Maybe you're a minister, but your parents wanted you to become a lawyer. Instead of attending law school, you went to Bible college, and it upset your parents. Twenty years later, they're still upset. You'll never be fully happy if you're always waiting for their approval. Find your approval in God, not in people, even if those people are close to you. Everyone hopes their father and mother value what they do, but many don't. What you eventually discover is that people who were messed up at nineteen are still messed up at sixty-seven. They don't outgrow it. They're consumed with themselves and their unhappiness. They should treat their children better, but they don't. Accept it and find satisfaction in knowing that God approves of what you're doing—as long as you're confident He does.

Peter and John said, *"Sirs, do you think we ought to please you rather than God? Let us clearly state, we would please God rather than men"* (Acts 5:29). Have that same attitude. People, even family, are entitled to their opinions, but you're free to do what's right and follow what you know to do in your spirit.

Stop wishing for other people's approval. The Bible warns, *"Beware when all men speak well of you"* (Luke 6:26). You should actually be concerned if everyone celebrates you. There are people whose approval you could easily gain by rejecting God's will for your life. If people are unhappy with you because you've chosen to follow God's calling, you should be fine with that—embrace their disapproval.

> Obviously, I'm not trying to win the approval of people, but of God. If pleasing people were my goal, I would not be Christ's servant.
>
> — GALATIANS 1:10 (NLT)

Don't seek disapproval, but don't compromise to gain approval.

DON'T ALLOW THE UNREALISTIC EXPECTATIONS OF OTHERS MAKE YOU UNHAPPY

Don't allow your happiness to be controlled by someone else. If you're waiting for your mother to apologize or for the person who impregnated you twenty years ago and never paid child support to come back and make things right, chances are it's not going to happen. So, forgive them and move on.

Stop wishing that someone would change into who you think they should be so you can be happy. It's not going to happen. People are who they are. I have no expectations for my daughter other than that she serves the Lord. You're not here to mold people into who you think they should be. You're not their Creator, so don't try to dictate what they do with their lives. Whatever you have a passion for is what you should pursue.

CHANGE 12

STOP MAGNIFYING THE MINUTE FAULTS OF THOSE CLOSE TO YOU

Magnifying the minute faults of someone close to you is a secret to *unhappiness*.

Don't complain that your husband sleeps until 11:00 a.m. every Saturday. He's probably tired. Let him sleep. Are you expecting him to wake up at 6:00 a.m. and make a quilt with you? Christian spousal complaints are the absolute lamest. "He works on that car in the garage every Saturday." Wow, you must be in line for a martyr's crown in Heaven for dealing with a man who works on his car every Saturday, along with the people who were beheaded in Egypt. I'll be praying for you. Marry someone with similar interests instead of marrying a guy who loves working on his car and expecting him to quilt with you.

Don't resent your husband for golfing every Saturday. He probably loves to golf. If you paid attention, you might have noticed that when you were dating him. Stop magnifying the minute faults of those close to you. Why complain when your husband sleeps late on Saturdays?

He could have a heroin problem—would you prefer that? If he golfs every Saturday, consider yourself blessed that he's not out visiting a mistress, like some husbands do. Which would you prefer? People need a release point: fishing, hunting, golfing, shopping, and playing video games provide a release. If it's legal and not a sin, leave people alone. Let them enjoy their hobbies.

Christians are professionals when it comes to magnifying small faults. Sometimes it's not even a fault, they just take an aspect of someone's life and beat them over the head with it. If something is sinful, it should be avoided, but if it's not a sin, there's no reason to feel bad about doing it. You shouldn't feel bad for doing something that relaxes you, and you shouldn't make someone feel bad for doing the same.

If your husband golfs every weekend, try buying a set of clubs and joining him. Stop magnifying minute faults—if they're even faults at all. I know I've provided several examples of wives who complain about their husbands, but I haven't often heard husbands complain about their wives' hobbies. Maybe they do, but they shouldn't either. Just stop making people feel bad for relaxing.

CHANGE 13

SEND SOMEONE A GIFT TODAY AND EVERY WEEK

Here are a couple of reasons why sending gifts is significant. It's something I started doing more consistently a few years ago. I've always sent gifts in the past, but now it's become a regular habit. Send someone a gift today, and do it every week.

1. THE LAW OF SOWING AND REAPING

If you want happiness, sow happiness, and you'll never lack it. Become an expert gift giver. I started sending people food this year—good food. Send gifts that people will remember twenty years from now. If you claim to not have money, that mindset will keep you from ever having it.

The cost of the gift doesn't matter. You can gift something from Amazon for ten bucks. You can DoorDash someone their favorite meal. Everyone likes food. It doesn't matter if you're rich, poor, or somewhere in between. When you notice someone likes something, bless them with it. It's the law of sowing and reaping—it's more blessed to give than to receive. When I preached day sessions at a friend's church, I bought Portillo's or Chick-fil-A for everyone. I didn't announce it ahead of time—I just surprised them. After the session, I'd let everyone know there were Chick-fil-A sandwiches for everyone in the back as a thank-you for coming to my meetings. I thought only those with less money would eat, but everyone did—business owners and men in suits were all equally thankful.

When you notice that someone likes something, it's an opportunity to bless them. What you sow, you reap. Instead of hoping for happiness from others, sow happiness into others. There's a euphoric release when you give a gift—it's a good feeling.

I remember buying an expensive watch for myself and then buying a more expensive one for someone else. When I bought the watch for myself, I thought, 'It looks nice. I could've used that money differently, but I needed a watch.' When I bought the watch for someone else—a pastor who used to be a chef—I couldn't wait to give it to him. He once mentioned that he'd wanted a watch but gave up on getting it when he entered the ministry. I made up my mind then, with only four hundred dollars in the bank, that I'd buy it for him as soon as I could. When I did, it cost about five thousand dollars, and I had fifty-eight hundred dollars in the bank at the time. I parted with most of my net worth to prove to him that serving the Lord brings more, not less. It's fun to give gifts.

My wife told me to stop buying her things. I enjoy it so much. I send steaks to pastors all over. I think I got it from my mother, she's a master gift-giver.

2. GIFT-GIVING BREAKS THE SPIRIT OF ENTITLEMENT

I didn't realize this when I started, but over the years I've noticed that non-givers often become entitled. They can list every person who didn't give them a good offering or who booked them a poor place to stay. If you're not a giver, you become entitled, but when you focus on giving, you stop keeping track of who owes you. You become focused on who you'll give to next. If you were to ask me the worst thing anyone's done to me in ministry, I wouldn't be able to tell you because I don't dwell on it. My mind is wired to think about who I can bless. Dwelling on past wrongs is a path to unhappiness. Becoming a giver breaks that cycle.

What Jesus said is true: What you make happen for others, God will make happen for you (Luke 6:38). Give to others, and God places a desire in others to give to you. You'll never need to manipulate people into giving. Be a blessing, and you'll never lack a blessing. It's rewarding to live in such a way that people smile when your name is mentioned. When God sees that you're that kind of person, He magnifies your ability to give.

> Knowing that whatsoever good thing any man doeth, the same shall he receive of the Lord, whether he be bond or free.
>
> — EPHESIANS 6:8

This principle overtakes every limitation. Even if you're a slave, God will bless you. Paul maintained his own home as a prisoner (Acts 28:30-31). Start a weekly gift-giving habit. It'll help *you* more than anyone else. You'll never be entitled. I don't know which pastors don't support my ministry—I only know the pastors I support. I don't know who doesn't give to me—I just know who I'm looking to give to. This habit breaks the greatest problem of our generation—entitlement.

Some people think God owes them. I don't feel that way about people or God. I don't dwell on unanswered prayers or on what more God could have done for me. My focus is on what more I can do for God and what else I can sacrifice to demonstrate my love for Him. God will bless me because it's His nature. If God never did another thing for me, or if He visited today and told me there's not enough room for me in Heaven, I'd still serve Him the same way. I love Him for who He is and for giving His Son. I love God's house. I love His Church. I love everything about Him.

> I speak not by commandment, but by occasion of the forwardness of others, and to prove the sincerity of your love.
>
> — 2 CORINTHIANS 8:8

3. GIVING PROVES THE SINCERITY OF YOUR LOVE

Love-fueled giving produces the fastest and most abundant results. God loves a cheerful giver. When your gift is an expression of your love, there's power in it. If you stay focused on being a blessing, happiness will never leave you. Financial giving brings financial harvests, but joy and happiness come along with it. The cheerfulness in giving brings a return of cheerfulness. I doubt there are any unhappy givers. I've never met one. Every unhappy person I know doesn't give.

Ask the Lord what would represent a true seed of gratitude and love for all He's done and sow it today. Just as remembering your wedding anniversary ensures you don't let a year pass without honoring your spouse. In the same way, honor God regularly with your giving. When was the last time you gave an Abraham-like offering to honor God? I hope you'll give that way for the rest of your life.

CHANGE 14

NEVER LEAVE YOUR CHARIOT TO CHASE A FOOL

As King David came to Bahurim, a man came out of the village cursing them. It was Shimei son of Gera, from the same clan as Saul's family. He threw stones at the king and the king's officers and all the mighty warriors who surrounded him. "Get out of here, you murderer, you scoundrel!" he shouted at David. "The Lord is paying you back for all the bloodshed in Saul's clan. You stole his throne, and now the Lord has given it to your son Absalom. At last you will taste some of your own medicine, for you are a murderer!" "Why should this dead dog curse my lord the king?" Abishai son of Zeruiah demanded. "Let me go over and cut off his head!" "No!" the king said. "Who asked your opinion, you sons of Zeruiah! If the Lord has told him to curse me, who are you to stop him?" Then David said to Abishai and to all his servants, "My own son is trying to kill me. Doesn't this relative of Saul have even more reason to do so? Leave him alone and let him curse, for the Lord has told him to do it. And perhaps the Lord will see that I am being wronged and will bless me because of these curses today." So David and his men continued down the road, and Shimei kept pace with them on a nearby hillside, cursing and throwing stones and dirt at David. The king and all who were with him grew weary along the way, so they rested when they reached the Jordan River.

— 2 SAMUEL 16:5-14 (NLT)

King David chose not to react to insults from Shimei. David knew that God could see and bless him for enduring his suffering. Never stop your chariot to chase a fool. David didn't allow someone else's actions to disrupt his peace. When someone suggested that David stop the chariot to cut off the head of a hater, David refused to stop and assumed God would bless him for listening to the insults.

Never stoop to the level of a fool. I've discussed this with my wife, Adalis. There are ministers who spend all day on Facebook arguing with people about Biden and Trump or pro-life versus pro-choice. You won't see Joel Osteen doing that. You never saw Billy Graham do it either. Social media wasn't around in David's time. Someone had to find you, throw dirt and rocks, and yell insults. That's what Shimei did. Nowadays, people just use social media to say rotten, untrue things. In David's day, they yelled in person. There are ways to handle these situations.

Post whatever you want on social media, and if people want to argue in the comments, let them. Part of the reason I started *Check the News* was to avoid posting twenty times a day and annoying people. Instead, I address everything in one broadcast. It's difficult to argue with someone actively broadcasting. Most people looking to pick a fight—the Shimeis of the world—won't take the time to watch an entire show.

When someone writes something inflammatory, your flesh wants to respond, but don't do it. X has a setting that only allows you to receive responses from accounts who follow you, so fly-by commenters don't appear. People who follow you are much less likely to write something unkind. If you're smart, you'll utilize that feature.

Avoid arguing with fools, especially if you pastor in a small town. It's a huge mistake. You might come up with a witty response, but you'll turn that person—and their friends and family—against you. In a small town, you can only argue so many times before you run out of people. If you're a pastor, keep track of the ratio of encouraging, spiritual posts to negative, controversial posts. Don't use social media to create conflict; stay immersed in what God called you to do. Never leave your chariot to chase a fool. Avoid arguing on social media. You cannot be a happy person while constantly engaged in conflict.

> But avoid foolish questions, and genealogies, and contentions, and strivings about the law; for they are unprofitable and vain.
>
> — TITUS 3:9

> And the servant of the Lord must not be quarrelsome; but be gentle unto all men, apt to teach, and patient.
>
> — 2 TIMOTHY 2:24

It's not that you can't fight—it's about choosing battles worth fighting. Fighting to have churches reopened while defending religious freedom is a fight worth having. I don't get worked up if a guy named Gary with a profile picture of Will Farrell from *Anchorman* thinks I'm a false prophet. I couldn't possibly care less what he thinks.

You can't be prone to arguing on social media and be a happy person. I was in Montreal when we first started live-streaming services. Someone posted three comments in all caps about what a horrible person I was. I was ready to respond, but I felt the Lord clearly speak to me: "If you do this, I'll keep you small for your own good. If one person's comment can steal your joy and occupy your time with back-and-forth arguments, I'll keep you small to protect you—it'll destroy you." I agreed with God, and He took away my tendency to be affected by what people say about me. Now, I don't care.

When you engage in arguments online, you send a reply and then wait for their response. You can't just compartmentalize it. It makes you short with your kids and your spouse. Don't do it. Don't let someone run out of a cave, yell at you, and steal your happiness. Never leave your chariot to chase a fool.

CHANGE 15

LOWER YOUR GOALS

Have you ever set out to read seven chapters of the Bible every day to read the Bible through in forty days? Then, find yourself struggling to keep up. Have you ever set an equally unrealistic goal? There's nothing wrong with committing to read one chapter each day. Make an achievable goal rather than an unrealistic goal that only leads to frustration and breeds unhappiness.

Instead of planning to work out four times a week for an hour, try three times a week for half an hour. Set a goal you can achieve. I'm not suggesting you give up on your dreams, but start with something manageable. Once you establish a routine, you can build on it.

When I started working out, I knew I hated going to the gym. I'm very good at *not* doing things, but I struggle with *doing* things. Fasting and prayer is a perfect example: fasting is easy for me—just don't eat. I find it effortless. Prayer, on the other hand, requires effort. Maybe that's why I've never smoked or drank alcohol. I was told I couldn't as a Christian, and I had no problem with that, but implementing things like physical exercise has always been a challenge.

I knew I needed to work out, so I booked a trainer. Not just for the training itself, but to create an appointment I couldn't cancel without disappointing someone. The accountability keeps me going. During the COVID lockdown, I tried at-home workout programs. I put one on in March and thought I would do it until the gyms opened back up. It was the first, last, and only time I did it until my gym reopened. Sooner or later, you need to discover who you are. Understand what you're not good at and adapt instead of constantly lying to yourself. Most people will not suddenly decide to wake up at 6:00 a.m. and pray for two hours. Start by waking up at 7:40 a.m. and praying for a focused twenty minutes.

When I started working out, I did it three times a week for half an hour. Once I got into a flow, I increased it to one-hour sessions every day I was home and even started doing it on the road. Start with lower goals to build a habit, then raise your goals gradually. Setting unrealistic goals leads to disappointment and unhappiness when you don't achieve them. Lower your goals and extend your deadlines. Setting a goal to finish writing a chapter of your next book by the end of today will breed stress. Instead, commit to completing it by the end of the week. Now you're relaxed, and you'll still get it done. If you can finish it by the end of the day, great, but if it's not coming together, give yourself more time. Likewise, setting a goal to clean the house by the end of the day creates a stressful day. Setting a goal to have it cleaned by a specific date alleviates stress.

CHANGE 16

TURN YOUR VEHICLE INTO A PLACE YOU ENJOY

Most people hate driving. I used to drive to all my meetings and only flew to a select few. If you manage your experience correctly, you'll actually feel sad when the drive is over. Turn your vehicle into a place you enjoy. Use the travel time to listen to preaching. Sometimes, I listen to audiobooks on my phone, and other times I listen to preaching, especially when I'm traveling to preach or I'm in the middle of meetings. When I take leisurely trips to Arizona with Adalis and Camila, I enjoy long drives of five hours or more. Driving in Arizona is very therapeutic for me—the scenery and a pair of sunglasses with high-quality lenses make everything look beautiful. Adalis usually falls asleep within ten minutes on the road, and Camila does the same. So I play an audiobook on topics I want to learn more about.

If you turn on Top 40 music or K-Love radio as background noise, you're wasting a large part of your life. Use that time to listen to something you're interested in, to learn something new, or to listen to preaching that builds your faith and knowledge of the Word.

You can transform your vehicle into a place you enjoy. Make it a learning space. Treat it like a daily seminar on the topics that interest you. One of the key differences between the rich and the poor is how they utilize their time in their vehicle.

When I preach in a town without nice places to stay, I book a place over forty minutes away. When I preached in Saskatchewan, there weren't nice places to stay in town, so my nephew, Jay, and I stayed an hour away. I treat that drive as study time. It's tempting to take the easy route and listen to an iTunes playlist, but that won't help you grow. Transform your vehicle into a learning space. Turn it into a place you truly enjoy.

CHANGE 17

LEARN TO CHANGE YOUR ATMOSPHERE

I've been asked to visit people's homes to pray for the sick. I did it more often when I was in my twenties while I was on the road at meetings. I noticed that depressed and sick people never had a happy atmosphere in their homes. It was as if the atmosphere in the house was conducive to sickness.

Take control of your atmosphere. I continue to apply this more and more. I knew an evangelist who would travel with all his own bedding in the trunk, strip the hotel bed, and replace it with his own bedding. He even traveled with pictures. He was on the road forty-six weeks of the year, so he would turn his hotel rooms into a home. Traveling for a week is one thing, but when you're gone for most of the year, it becomes your life. He transformed his atmosphere into what he wanted it to be. I thought it was crazy at the time, but I understand why he did it now. He was creating a happy atmosphere.

Here are four things you can do to change your atmosphere.

CONTROL WHAT YOU SMELL

You don't really know how your house smells because you spend so much time there, but visitors notice how someone's house smells. The smell of your house probably won't bother you, but when it smells great, it makes a difference. It's not about spending a lot of money. How much does a candle cost? You don't need to be a millionaire to buy a candle or spray a fragrance you enjoy. Buy a candle and choose a great scent.

In some countries, they don't like wearing deodorant. I was on an international flight with someone who felt this way, and the whole plane stunk. You could decide you hate flying to an entire country because most people don't wear deodorant, or you could make a change. I went to L'Occitane and had them make me a custom potent fragrance. When I boarded the plane, I sprayed it in the air. I don't know if you're allowed to do that, but I figured if people are allowed to blast their scent, why can't I? I sprayed it, and it totally overtook the smell of the plane. About an hour later, I gave the plane a refresher, and I controlled the smell of the flight.

CONTROL WHAT YOU SEE

What do you have on your walls? At twenty-four, if you would have told me that the day would come when I'd order art for my home, I'd have said you were out of your mind, but here we are. My favorite site on planet Earth might be Bell Rock in Sedona, Arizona. So, I bought the largest quality portrait I could find and hung it up in our living room. It's in my line of vision every time I sit in my spot. It makes me happy every time I look at it.

You might think I'm out of my mind, but even my favorite mug makes me happy. I bought it at a resort called The Phoenician in Scottsdale, Arizona, my favorite place to stay. I've been there with Adalis and Camila. Just looking at that mug brings back memories of being there with my daughter and wife. Take control of your atmosphere. Make things the way you want them. If something is bothering you, change it.

CONTROL WHAT YOU HEAR

Anointed music changes an atmosphere. Don't let the television dictate the atmosphere in your home. One good thing that came out of COVID was that all the commercials about staying home, washing your hands, and wearing a mask irritated me so much that I stopped watching television. I still play video games almost every day when I'm home, but I haven't watched television in a long time. Those public service ads insisting everyone wear a mask when they go outside—that's not joy. I don't need to be reminded of terminal disease during every commercial break.

I don't allow people I'd never invite into my home to determine its atmosphere. Reality television is built on arguing, and I don't allow arguing in my home. We don't argue, and I don't want to listen to people arguing on television. It's not relaxing or joyful.

You can't watch something and expect it not to have an effect on you. When you watch people argue on TV, it will affect how you deal with conflict. You'll become quicker tempered. Everything is received through impartation.

Don't allow other people to dictate the atmosphere in your home. Your home needs to be a nest without thorns. It should be a place you enjoy spending time, and it's your job to create that space. Put speakers around your property or in your house and play anointed music.

When Saul was tormented, he summoned David to play the harp. David was so anointed that the spirit tormenting Saul left him. Today, you don't need a harpist—all you need is a Bluetooth speaker and a cell phone. You can afford a Bluetooth speaker to dictate the sounds in your home. The key is to develop a mindset to pursue and maintain the happiness that God offers you.

CONTROL WHAT YOU SPEAK

Speak the right words until the right feelings form. This is the key to immediately changing your mood. Most people think their mood is a roll of the dice or a spin of the wheel. You can put yourself in a good mood by speaking the right words until your emotions align with your speech. It's never something you'll feel like doing. If you're angry about something, you'll feel like calling someone to vent your anger, but that never makes you feel better—it just causes you to dwell on that feeling. If you feel depressed, you'll naturally want to listen to music that feeds your depression.

> Bless the Lord, O my soul, and forget not all His benefits: Who forgives all your iniquities, Who heals all your diseases, Who redeems your life from destruction, Who crowns you with lovingkindness and tender mercies, Who

satisfies your mouth with good *things, So that* your youth is renewed like the eagle's.

— PSALM 103:2-5 (NKJV)

Your mind is not your master—your mind is your servant. The same applies to your emotions. My body chemistry does not get to tell me how I'm going to feel. I've made up my mind to be happy. If feelings of unhappiness come, remember what Kenneth Hagin used to say about thoughts: "You can't stop a bird from flying over your head, but you can keep it from building a nest in your hair." It's the same with feelings. You can't stop feelings from coming, but you don't have to build a home for them. Shake it off. You only have so many days on this Earth, and you don't have enough time to waste even one day being depressed, sad, or dwelling on hurt.

Try saying the opposite of what you're feeling by substituting words from the Bible. When you're upset, what if you said this? "Thank You, Father. The joy of the Lord is my strength." Did you know the Devil is a created being? He doesn't know how you feel until you tell him. So use your words to frustrate him. If he tries to make you feel depressed, say, "Father, I thank You for joy, unspeakable and full of glory."

Are you worried about a business contract or money? Say, "Thank You, Father, that as I obey You, You said You'll open the windows of Heaven and pour out a blessing so great I won't have enough room to take it all in. Thank ou that Your Word cannot be altered."

Talk like that for two or three minutes, and see how you feel afterward. Use your mouth. Death and life are in the power of the tongue.

Oral Roberts used to always say, "Something good is going to happen to me today." Now you practice saying this, "Thank You, Father, that You said in Your Word, surely goodness and mercy will follow me all the days of my life."

CHANGE 18

REMOVE THE REBELLIOUS IMMEDIATELY

David did not stop his chariot so the caveman in 2 Samuel 16 could continue shouting at him, but he didn't hire him either. This principle doesn't apply to your family, but for business owners, pastors, or anyone in leadership, it's important to act. Remove anyone who is rebellious if they are not part of your immediate family. If your mother-in-law tries to incite rebellion in your spouse, keep your distance. You can call them on Mother's Day, but don't let them have a significant place in your life. Even so, when David's son, Absalom, rebelled, David dealt with him. Address rebellion *immediately*. Some Christians would do well to watch *The Godfather* I and II several times and take notes, because rebellion must be taken seriously. Anyone who rises up against your leadership must be dealt with severely.

Pastors tolerate rebellion far too often. A worship leader who refuses to sing the songs the pastor requests is rebellious. There's nothing to pray about; they should be removed immediately. Pastors who allow rebellion end up being voted out of their own churches. You don't need to ask God how to navigate the situation when the Bible already provides a clear blueprint for dealing with rebellion. I would play a CD for praise and worship before allowing a rebellious worship leader to stand on the platform and refuse to submit to my leadership. This isn't just about ministry—the same applies to business owners.

Keep in mind the roles of the Great Shepherd, the under-shepherd, sheep, wolves, and wolves in sheep's clothing. Not everyone who crosses your path is there to be rehabilitated. If someone walks into one of my meetings with a ski mask and a gun, their eternal destiny is not my concern—the safety of the congregation is. They will be dealt with harshly, and I'll sleep like a baby that night knowing I dealt appropriately with a wolf. A shepherd doesn't try to turn a wolf into a sheep—a shepherd defends the sheep from the wolf.

If you deal with a rebellious person on your staff right away, only the rebellious person leaves. If you allow them to stay, they will influence others and build a following, which could lead to a church split. The difference between an individual leaving a church and a church split is often determined by the length of time the pastor allows a rebellious person to remain.

Some people have said things to their pastors that, if it were said in my ministry, they wouldn't have finished the sentence before they were fired. Rebellion is a demonic trait. It's what caused Satan to be thrown out of Heaven. Satan's desire to ascend and be like the Most High caused him to overstep his God-ordained role. Rebellion is a satanic attribute, not a godly one—so deal with it. Don't wait for problems to resolve themselves. Remove them. Problems don't start big—they start small. If you address them when they're small, they'll never grow large.

Some churches are experiencing rapid growth while others suffer a huge drop off in attendance, some even on the brink of closing, and it's all based on how the leader handled COVID. It's not just about whether they shut down or stayed open. Leaders faced factions within their churches. Some threatened to leave if they didn't reopen. Others claimed they would never return if the church reopened too soon. Some refused to wear masks to church, and others claimed mask mandates must be enforced for them to return. It all stemmed from a lack of decisive leadership, that allowed rebellion to form and led to major problems. If leaders had simply asserted a course of action, the divisions could have been avoided.

Rebellion is not always overt. Openly questioning leadership in front of others is an act of rebellion. I once knew a pastor who planned to host several members of my family for events in the same year. One of his staff members remarked, "Wow, you've really been baptized into the Shuttlesworths this year," in front of several people. That type of behavior has never occurred in my ministry, and it never will. Being anointed comes with the added benefit of sensing when someone develops an issue before it becomes problematic. While I make an effort to avoid hiring such individuals, if an incident like that were to occur, it would only happen once because a shiver would be sent down the spine of each person present to witness my response to such rebellion.

The U.S. military is one of the most powerful forces on Earth because it understands authority and submission. If a general announces an attack at 0500 hours, a captain doesn't question whether it's a good idea—he would be finished. The Kingdom of God operates on a similar structure of authority. When Peter told Jesus to stop talking about going to Jerusalem, Jesus looked at the other disciples and then responded to Peter by saying, "Get thee behind me, Satan" (Matthew 16:22-28). Public questioning received a public rebuke. Leaders who fail to address rebellion will have small, stagnant ministries or businesses.

One pastor I knew was an excellent, anointed preacher, but he never dealt with his rebellious staff. He built his church to three hundred and fifty people, but he allowed a staff member to openly question his leadership, gain a following, and take two hundred and fifty people out of his church. Then he started again with eighty, built it up to three hundred and fifty, and the same thing happened again and again. It must have happened five times, and now he's retired. There's nothing holy, spiritual, or Christ-like about allowing a rebellious person to destroy your life. Remove the rebellious immediately. It's a demonic attitude.

CHANGE 19

REMOVE LIARS IMMEDIATELY

If you catch someone in a lie, remember the Bible speaks against confronting them directly. Liars often become defensive or aggressive, like a rabid pit bull. Instead, just nod your head and get rid of them.

 Anyone who will lie to you will also steal from you.

> But there was a certain man named Ananias who, with his wife, Sapphira, sold some property. He brought part of the money to the apostles, claiming it was the full amount. With his wife's consent, he kept the rest. Then Peter said, "Ananias, why have you let Satan fill your heart? You lied to the Holy Spirit, and you kept some of the money for yourself. The property was yours to sell or not sell, as you wished. And after selling it, the money was also yours to give away. How could you do a thing like this? You weren't

lying to us but to God!" As soon as Ananias heard these words, he fell to the floor and died. Everyone who heard about it was terrified. Then some young men got up, wrapped him in a sheet, and took him out and buried him. About three hours later his wife came in, not knowing what had happened. Peter asked her, "Was this the price you and your husband received for your land?" "Yes," she replied, "that was the price." And Peter said, "How could the two of you even think of conspiring to test the Spirit of the Lord like this? The young men who buried your husband are just outside the door, and they will carry you out, too." Instantly, she fell to the floor and died. When the young men came in and saw that she was dead, they carried her out and buried her beside her husband. Great fear gripped the entire church and everyone else who heard what had happened.

— ACTS 5:1-11 (NLT)

God hates lying. Lying is a serious matter to God. It's one of the only reasons He killed someone post-resurrection. God killed Ananias and Sapphira for lying about their offering. People tried to kill the apostles, and God didn't strike them dead, but when a husband and wife lied about their offering, the Holy Ghost questioned them about it, and they lied brazenly. Peter also took lying seriously. After Ananias died and his wife Sapphira came waltzing in, he asked the same question again.

God is consistent. He despised lying in the Old Testament as well.

When Gehazi, Elisha's servant, lied about accepting gifts from Naaman, he was struck with leprosy as a result.

> But Gehazi, the servant of Elisha, the man of God, said to himself, "My master should not have let this Aramean get away without accepting any of his gifts. As surely as the Lord lives, I will chase after him and get something from him." So Gehazi set off after Naaman. When Naaman saw Gehazi running after him, he climbed down from his chariot and went to meet him. "Is everything all right?" Naaman asked. "Yes," Gehazi said, "but my master has sent me to tell you that two young prophets from the hill country of Ephraim have just arrived. He would like 75 pounds of silver and two sets of clothing to give to them." "By all means, take twice as much silver," Naaman insisted. He gave him two sets of clothing, tied up the money in two bags, and sent two of his servants to carry the gifts for Gehazi. But when they arrived at the citadel, Gehazi took the gifts from the servants and sent the men back. Then he went and hid the gifts inside the house. When he went in to his master, Elisha asked him, "Where have you been, Gehazi?" "I haven't been anywhere," he replied. But Elisha asked him, "Don't you realize that I was there in spirit when Naaman stepped down from his chariot to meet you? Is this the time to receive money and clothing, olive groves and vineyards, sheep and cattle, and male and female servants? Because you have done this, you and your descendants will suffer from Naaman's leprosy forever." When Gehazi left the

room, he was covered with leprosy; his skin was white as snow.

— 2 KINGS 5:20-27 (NLT)

Revelation 21:8 includes liars on the list of people who will be thrown into the lake of fire. Take lying seriously and remove any liars from your life.

Get rid of liars. Don't employ them. Take lying seriously. If someone lies about small matters, they'll lie about larger ones. Our ministry changed CPAs once we found out the Christian CPA we were using turned out to be a liar. He claimed to have 1.2 million social media followers. He would tweet something and receive one retweet and one like. All his followers were bots—fake followers that could be purchased. When they cracked down on it, his follower count dropped dramatically. He was a liar, and that was only one of the things he lied about. Why would I trust someone who lies on social media to account for our ministry's money? I got rid of him immediately. Misrepresenting yourself is lying. People claim they're reaching millions of people on television every day. Just because the channel your program is on is available in millions of homes, doesn't mean millions are watching you. That's lying. I hate it with a passion, in case you haven't noticed.

A minister I know helped a man in his congregation find a job. One morning, while praying in his office, he felt the Lord speak to him: "He's not going to that job you got for him. He doesn't show up." He called the man during work hours and asked him where he was. The man claimed to be at work and thanked the pastor again for getting him the job. The preacher drove to the man's house and knocked on the door. The man opened the door in his pajamas, surrounded by food and popcorn with the television on.

"Oh, Pastor," the man said nervously.

"I thought you said you were at work," the pastor replied.

"Well, I haven't been going," the man sheepishly responded.

"You're a liar," the preacher stated.

I would never help someone like that again. I would have nothing to do with them—just outright lying to a preacher. Keep your word. If you tell someone you'll be somewhere, honor that commitment. Don't be the type of person who doesn't show up and texts the next day with an excuse. Be dependable and truthful.

CHANGE 20

FIND SOMEONE OR SOMETHING THAT MAKES YOU LAUGH AND LISTEN OR WATCH IT EVERY DAY

A merry heart doeth good like a medicine: but a broken spirit drieth the bones.

— PROVERBS 17:22

No one has ever joyfully asked me to keep them in prayer; with every attack comes the oppression that sustains it. Like a fish that can't survive outside of water, an oppressive spirit and an oppressive attack cannot survive in an atmosphere of joy and laughter.

For some of you reading, *Check the News* is what you watch to laugh every day. That's what it was designed to do. We mock the plans of the Devil live on air. We don't worry about what he's planning. You have the victory, and you will keep it. No one has the power to take your victory or your joy away from you.

Find someone or something that makes you laugh and listen to or watch it every day. There are people I watch who are not very spiritual. They're not inappropriate, but they're not Christians. They're funny, so I listen to them. I've noticed that when I tried to drive through the night, I would rely on coffee or Red Bull to help me stay awake, but I found that nothing keeps me awake and alert better than listening to something that makes me laugh hard. Joy brings strength.

There's a great minister who is used mightily in the power of God. I once visited his home, expecting to find him praying or engaged in some serious activity, especially having just finished a week of meetings. When I walked in, he was watching *The Three Stooges*, lying on the floor next to his couch and laughing so hard that his belly shook. I learned a valuable lesson: you can be an anointed, holy person and still indulge in laughter. Find something that makes you laugh.

CHANGE 21

KEEP PAINFUL MEMORIES IN A PLACE YOU CAN ACCESS WHEN YOU'RE READY

I once visited someone's home and saw a large black-and-white portrait of a little girl around two years old. They explained it was a picture of their daughter, who passed away when she was a year and a half. It would be cruel and unhealthy to never think about your daughter ever again, but it's equally unhealthy to put a huge picture of such a painful memory in a prominent place like the living room, where you look at it every day. Anytime happiness comes, her memory acts as a trigger to pull you back into the most painful event of your life. If you've lost someone close to you, don't burn all the photos or refuse to talk about them. Some react that way, and it isn't healthy. Instead, keep the pictures somewhere where you can see your loved one who passed away when you're in the proper mood and you're strong.

For instance, if your boss told you you're getting a one-thousand-dollar bonus, your first instinct might be to celebrate and text a friend, but if your phone's background is a picture of the person you lost, that happiness can quickly turn to sadness.

Display pictures of your most joyful moments. If you catch sight of a painful photo when you're in a good mood, it can feel like a punch to the stomach. At the same time, if you see a picture of the best day you've ever had, you could be in a bad mood and look up at it out of the blue, and it will snap you out of the bad mood. Use it to your advantage.

Place Pictures in Your House of Things, Places, People, and Memories That Make You Smile

The mug I bought at a resort just outside Phoenix, Arizona, makes me happy. It was one of the best trips I've ever taken, and seeing it reminds me of that. Keep things in your line of sight that lift your mood.

Some people, including speakers and leaders, base their lives around their tragedies, and it's clear they haven't fully healed. Don't base your life on a tragedy—base your life on the promises of God and faith for the great things God has for your future. Remember, pictures naturally depict the past—you can't take photos of the future.

Avoid putting yourself in a situation where you are constantly reminded of grief. Keep painful memories in a special place where you're not forced to look at them. Don't make yourself relive the worst day of your life every day. Display photos that capture the happiest moments of your life. Just as some pictures can trigger painful memories, others can bring joy. Photos cause memories to flood back into your mind. Fill your space with images that remind you of victories and joyful times, not defeats. Keep in sight things that lift you emotionally. Don't dwell on defeat—focus on victories.

CHANGE 22

FIND A WAY TO DO WHAT YOU LOVE MOST FOR A LIVING

This might be the most potent of all the changes to immediately improve your happiness: Find a way to begin doing what you love most for a living. It's an old but true cliché: if you do what you love, you'll never work a day in your life. Instead of planning a vacation, build a life that you don't want to take a break from. I could preach and broadcast every day for the rest of my life. The only reason I take a break is because it's biblical and because I want to spend time with my wife and daughter.

When Adalis and I started two churches in Hawaii on the island of Maui, one of the young kids, now a man in his early twenties, started coming to the meetings and gave his life to the Lord. I follow him on Instagram, and though he rarely posts, he loves to hunt. He posted a picture of himself carrying a pig on his back after a boar hunt in Maui. In the photo, he's shirtless, wearing shorts, carrying the boar out of the forest. He wrote a long post about how much he loves hunting and how he could do it every day. If I were him, I would start a YouTube channel that featured his hunting expeditions. Then, I'd seek sponsorships and chart a course to take that show to the Outdoor Channel or buy a Saturday slot on Hawaiian television.

It may be that you can't necessarily drop everything you're doing right now to pursue what you love, but you can start moving in that direction today. Willie George—some of you know him as Gospel Bill—pastored one of the greatest churches in America. He would do a series every year that people loved. It focused on developing a "sixth-day project." God said six days of the week are for work. The Western system is a five-day workweek, with a day to relax, followed by the Lord's Day. What if, instead of working five days and spending Saturday watching college football or binge watching Netflix, you dedicated Saturday to *your* project? Show God that you can be your own boss. Take initiative without anyone pushing you. Most people struggle with self-motivation when there's no one yelling at them, docking their pay, or giving them a warning. When they're in an environment where no one cares whether they work or not, most people choose to chill. It requires a different kind of drive to be successful in these situations.

Show the Lord that you can take a free day and start a project that could eventually become more significant than your current job instead of letting your flesh do what it wants. Decide to take your sixth day to start a project that will eventually overwhelm your current career. If you're happy in your current job like I am, then this doesn't apply. I love ministering the Word of God, teaching, and preaching. While many evangelists dislike travel, I've learned to enjoy it. I made up my mind: if I'm going to travel for sixty years, I won't complain about any aspect of travel. I've found ways to make it fun, which has been challenging, but you won't to do something you hate your whole life. When your joy stops, make a change. You must keep what you do fun, or you'll quit.

Ask yourself these questions: What could I read about for hours without noticing how much time has flown by? What do I enjoy doing so much that time escapes you? For me, it's preaching. You only have one life. Why not spend it doing what you're passionate about instead of working just to pay bills? Sales jobs are fine, and some people love them. If you're in sales, why not write down what you've learned and create a book? Bring elements of your job into your domain.

 Your passion is a clue as to what you're wired to do. What you love doing isn't an accident.

Find a way to begin doing what you love most for a living. If I loved fixing classic cars, I'd start with one and make a YouTube channel. There are many ways to make money doing what you love that weren't possible before. People make a living playing video games—not because they're experts, but because they are entertaining while playing. They start YouTube channels or Twitch streams, build audiences, earn sponsorships, and hundreds of thousands of dollars a year.

Don't focus on your limitations or what you don't have. If you want to take the YouTube route, don't worry about sponsors, just start. I remember hearing ministers discuss Benny Hinn and claim they could do a lot if they had a jet like him. No one handed Benny Hinn a jet—he put his faith out for one. Lose the *it-must-be-nice* mentality.

As a Christian, you can combine action with Scripture and pray, "Father, You said whatever I put my hand to, You would bless. I know You're not a stupid God. I know You're the all-wise God. If *I* know I need a sponsor, *You* know I need sponsorship for this program. I pray You will make it happen." When you put it in God's hands, there's no need to badger people. He'll put you in the path of someone who will help you and show you how to make it work. That's how God steps in. You make a plan, and God will help you fulfill it.

Make a list of what you need and start moving forward. The Bible says, *"Despise not the day of small beginnings, for it delights the Lord to see the work begin"* (Zechariah 4:10). A task can appear overwhelming when you look at the whole thing, but if you break it into pieces and make a list, you can begin having faith for it. Calculate the expenses for the equipment associated with your dream and set your faith to acquire what you need. When you break your big dream into accomplishable steps, God will help you as you take the steps. Reinhard Bonnke used to say, "God moves with the movers. God goes with the goers. He doesn't sit with the sitters." God looks for people who will move. Everyone starts somewhere. Focus on where you're going and ask God to bless it. Then move in that direction like you believe God will do it.

There's a way to monetize whatever you love. If you love to fight, find a way to make money while doing it. If you love talking about fantasy football or college football, pursue a career in it. You'll be very happy. Pay attention to what flows out of you like a river. People make their living by opening gifts sent to them on Instagram. People pay to watch them open gifts. Don't tell me there's no way to do what you love for a living; you're not using your brain if you aren't monetizing your passion. If you take the time to watch people who are successful in your field of interest, you'll notice that they're just humans like you. What separates people is not their talent—it's the decisions they make to develop and monetize their talent.

CHANGE 23

DO WHAT YOU DO YOUR WAY

David asked the soldiers standing nearby, "What will a man get for killing this Philistine and ending his defiance of Israel? Who is this pagan Philistine anyway, that he is allowed to defy the armies of the living God?" And these men gave David the same reply. They said, "Yes, that is the reward for killing him." But when David's oldest brother, Eliab, heard David talking to the men, he was angry. "What are you doing around here anyway?" he demanded. "What about those few sheep you're supposed to be taking care of? I know about your pride and deceit. You just want to see the battle!"

— 1 SAMUEL 17:26-28 (NLT)

Satan's primary strategy to discourage you from pursuing what God has called you to do or from undertaking something significant is through personal attack. When someone hurls insults at you, claiming you're prideful and deceitful, that's an accusation. Accusation is not a godly quality—it's a satanic one. Satan is called the "accuser of the brethren." Anytime someone behaves that way, they are inspired by the Devil. Nobody speaking by the Holy Ghost would ever make accusations against you. If you take those accusations to heart, they'll keep you from doing what God has called you to do.

If something is on your heart, do it. You'll face criticism for doing nothing, and you'll face it for doing something. If David hadn't fought Goliath, his brother probably would have complained that he stayed with the sheep where it was safe and called him a coward. Don't allow people's opinions to dictate your actions. Follow what God has placed in your heart and do it the way He has instructed you to.

> Then David's question was reported to King Saul, and the king sent for him. "Don't worry about this Philistine," David told Saul. "I'll go fight him!" "Don't be ridiculous!" Saul replied. "There's no way you can fight this Philistine and possibly win! You're only a boy, and he's been a man of war since his youth."
>
> — 1 SAMUEL 17:31-33 (NLT)

The next challenge you'll face is discouragement. People will come up with all kinds of reasons why you're not qualified to do what God has called you to do, but if God has called you, He has qualified and equipped you for it.

> But David persisted. "I have been taking care of my father's sheep and goats," he said. "When a lion or a bear comes

to steal a lamb from the flock, I go after it with a club and rescue the lamb from its mouth. If the animal turns on me, I catch it by the jaw and club it to death. I have done this to both lions and bears, and I'll do it to this pagan Philistine, too, for he has defied the armies of the living God! The Lord who rescued me from the claws of the lion and the bear will rescue me from this Philistine!" Saul finally consented. "All right, go ahead," he said. "And may the Lord be with you!"

Then Saul gave David his own armor—a bronze helmet and a coat of mail. David put it on, strapped the sword over it, and took a step or two to see what it was like, for he had never worn such things before. "I can't go in these," he protested to Saul. "I'm not used to them." So David took them off again. He picked up five smooth stones from a stream and put them into his shepherd's bag. Then, armed only with his shepherd's staff and sling, he started across the valley to fight the Philistine.

— 1 SAMUEL 17:34-40 (NLT)

Don't allow the Eliabs and Sauls of life to keep you small. I once heard something that stuck with me. Jerry Seinfeld, the famous comedian, was on David Letterman's *Late Night* talk show. Letterman congratulated Seinfeld on his success, and Seinfeld thanked Letterman in return. "Thank me for what?" Letterman asked, surprised. Seinfeld explained that the last time he came on Letterman's show, he was preparing to launch *Seinfeld*, and Letterman gave him advice that made all the difference. Letterman was still clueless, so Seinfeld reminded him, "You told me the network executives would try to change my show into something different from what I envisioned. 'Don't let them do it. If you're going to fail, fail your way.'"

If you're going to fail, fail your way. That's what David did. People warned him the giant would kill him. King Saul offered David his armor, but David knew if he was going to die, he was going to die fighting his way. As it turned out, if David had used Saul's armor, Goliath would have slain him easily. He knew how to fight soldiers in armor. Goliath had a massive shield and sword, but David knew how to use a slingshot—a skill Goliath knew nothing about.

When the Devil realizes he can't deter you, he'll try to turn you into a vanilla version of yourself. He'll try to strip away the unique gifts and abilities God placed in you that make you different. You'll be criticized for your differences, but it's your differences that make you unique and hold the key to your success.

 You get criticized for your differences, but it's your differences that make you unique and hold the key to your success.

"Jonathan, you shouldn't stand on chairs when you preach, pastors won't like that"

"You shout too much."

"You should try to keep your sermons to thirty-five minutes."

If I had taken everyone's advice over the years, there'd be no reason to listen to me because there'd be a million preachers just like me, who all finish in thirty-five minutes, pace around, and speak at a reasonable decibel. There'd be nothing to set me apart. The things that make you different are the keys to your success.

If you write like everybody else writes, who needs to read what you write? If Adalis had married another preacher, they would have ruined her. Most ministers would have insisted she stop flailing her arms around and told her to quit using the word "freakin" every fifteen minutes. They would have reprimanded her for pulling out an AR-15 from under the table and gesturing with it on camera. You're not going to turn Adalis into Queen Elizabeth, and you shouldn't try. There are enough women on Christian television who "settle down." There's nothing wrong with having one Puerto Rican who's flailing and different. There are many women teachers and preachers, but there's no one like Adalis. There might be someone you like better, but no one could claim to be like her. She doesn't try to be unique—she is unique. She's a Puerto Rican redneck with an NRA backpack, and it confuses people into listening to what she has to say. Before they know it, they're interested in hearing more about God's Word.

I pay close attention to what my daughter loves, and I don't try to rewire her interests to match mine. One day, Camila and I were watching Christian Television, and she asked, "Dad, why doesn't that guy talk about Jesus?" I didn't know. She said, "I'm going to make a YouTube channel called *Camila Really Talks About Jesus*." If she takes an interest in preaching, I won't push her to do it the way I do, because I've been trying not to preach like myself. The Bible says there are different gifts and administrations but the same Spirit. Even if you're in the same field as someone else, you don't have to be a carbon copy. My dad is a preacher and has three brothers who are also preachers, and they're all very different.

Your uniqueness is what sets you apart, which is why the world tries to strip it away. Do what you do the way you do it. If you're going to fail, fail your way. I dress how I want, and I preach how I preach. I want to look a certain way to represent the Kingdom of God. You're free to dress how you want, but I won't strip away what God put in me that makes me different just to fit a mold. That's what religion does—everyone looks the same, preaches the same, and has the same haircut. In some denominations, everyone seems like a clone. Some even scratch their heads the same way at the same time.

There's something God placed in you that causes you to stand out. It's obvious just by looking that God doesn't want everyone to look the same. God loves variety. A Nigerian doesn't look anything like someone from Finland. God did that on purpose. Think of how He created Heaven. The gates are made up of different gemstones. I bet you Heaven won't be a static place. There'll be something new all the time. God loves you exactly the way He made you. There's no need to speak in a different tone of voice when you pray. God knows how you sound.

I used to think I needed to stop joking around to be a preacher. When I attended Bible college, I told myself I would stop joking around. I decided I would be a very serious and stern person. Then I realized my humor is a gift. Most people don't have anyone who makes them laugh. Bringing joy to people isn't unholy. Don't reject what makes you unique.

CHANGE 24

STOP SINNING

Sin shall not have dominion over you.

— ROMANS 6:14

Sin brings sorrow, emotional pain, and opens the door to depression. Even if sin brings temporary pleasure to your flesh, that fleeting satisfaction is quickly replaced by overwhelming grief. You often hear people who aren't even Christians say things like, "I'm never drinking again." No one comes out of sin saying, "I want to do that more." Instead, there's a regret because, deep inside, they can feel themselves dying. *The wages of sin is death* (Romans 6:23).

> When you follow the desires of your sinful nature, the results are very clear: sexual immorality, impurity, lustful pleasures, idolatry, sorcery, hostility, quarreling, jealousy, outbursts of anger, selfish ambition, dissension, division, envy, drunkenness, wild parties, and other sins like

these. Let me tell you again, as I have before, that anyone living that sort of life will not inherit the Kingdom of God.

— GALATIANS 5:19-21 (NLT)

Everything listed in the scriptures above should be removed from your life permanently. You'll never find happiness living in sin. It leads to an eternity in Hell.

It took me over twenty years of doing my best to get where I am now. Not that I'm the picture of success, but I have reached a point where I have experienced significant breakthrough. I could throw all that away in an instant—I've seen it happen to others. I'll never abandon it all because the fruitfulness of what God called me to do is my greatest source of pleasure.

The misery that comes from sin will always overwhelm whatever temporary satisfaction it brings you. Stop sinning and slam the door on unhappiness. If you're living with someone you're not married to, leave today. Throw out the alcohol in your home right now. Get rid of sin, or it will get rid of you, because sin destroys everything it touches. It's a long road back from sin; it eats away at progress. It's never worth it. You don't have enough time on Earth to throw your life away for sin.

If you need to receive Jesus Christ and repent of sin, it starts with saying, "Father, I'm sorry. I'm done with this. Give me the power to change." Get rid of sin today and slam the door on the Devil's ability to make you unhappy.

AFTERWORD

You don't have to choose between taking up your cross, having joy, winning souls, or experiencing health and wealth. Some people claim American preachers talk about health and wealth when it should be all about souls, but how many souls can you win if you're unhappy, impoverished, and sick?

You can have *everything* God promised. Imagine the Bible as a big buffet: *"I'll prepare a table before you in the presence of your enemies"* (Psalm 23:5). Picture God preparing a spread for you with plates of healing, joy, happiness, prosperity, peace, and land ownership. As Kenneth Hagin once said, "God didn't fill His book with useless statements or things of minor importance."

You can have everything God says is yours in His Word. You can win souls and still be happy. You can create happiness for your family. Most Christians are miserable people. They love God, read His Word, and pray, but they aren't happy. I've heard messages about why joy is essential but happiness isn't. That doesn't make sense to me. Who has joy and is unhappy? Your joy should produce happiness, and with God's wisdom, you should organize your life to live happily. Joy comes from the Holy Spirit and from knowing your sins are forgiven. Happiness is temporal, but while you're on this Earth, you should structure your life in a way that makes you happy. Some things are within your control. Let's get to the bottom of it: What's making you unhappy?

> "This command I am giving you today is not too difficult for you, and it is not beyond your reach. It is not kept in heaven, so distant that you must ask, 'Who will go up to heaven and bring it down so we can hear it and obey?' It is not kept beyond the sea, so far away that you must ask, 'Who will cross the sea to bring it to us so we can hear it and obey?' No, the message is very close at hand; it is on your lips and in your heart so that you can obey it. 'Now listen! Today I am giving you a choice between life and death, between prosperity and disaster."
>
> — DEUTERONOMY 30:11-15 (NLT)

God gave us a choice. If you don't choose prosperity, you're choosing disaster.

Choose blessing,

Choose prosperity.

Choose life.

Choose happiness.

If you don't chart a course for your life, others will chart it for you.

AFTERWORD

Remember being a child, waking up in the summer with endless possibilities? As you grow, responsibilities are added, but you are still responsible for your choices. You don't have to lose that outlook on life. When you wake up, you can do whatever you want. When you stand before God, He won't say, "Sorry, all that happened to you." He will hold you accountable for the decisions you made. *"Oh, that you would choose life so that you and your descendants might live"* (Deuteronomy 30:19 NLT). I choose life, prosperity, blessing, and happiness. Happiness is a biblical synonym for blessing.

> Happy is he that hath the God of Jacob for his help, whose hope is in the Lord his God.
>
> — PSALM 146:5

Happiness is scriptural and a product of your decisions. Take control of your life. If you don't like where you work, change it. You chose to work there; you can choose not to work there anymore. Life, happiness, and joy are choices. Life is a choice. Remaining in depression is a choice because the Bible shows you how to break free. The Bible is a book of choices. *"As for me and my house, we will serve the Lord"* (Joshua 24:15). Choosing to repent instead of harboring sin is a choice. Forgiving someone who hurt you instead of holding onto unforgiveness is a decision. God didn't institute forgiveness to help those receiving it, but to keep joyful people free from bitterness.

So, choose joy. Choose happiness. Choose life. If you've never received Jesus Christ as your Lord and Savior, that's where happiness begins. Oh, the joy of those whose sins are forgiven! You can begin improving your happiness by accepting Jesus as your Savior by openly and honestly praying this aloud before God:

Heavenly Father,
I know I've sinned, and I need Your forgiveness. Today, I'm done with my old way of living. I believe Jesus died for my sins and rose again to give me life. Right now, I turn my back on sin, and I give my life to You. Jesus, come into my heart. Be my Savior, my Lord, and my best friend. Fill me with Your Holy Spirit so I can live for You—strong, bold, and happy every day of my life. Thank You for loving me and saving me. From this moment, I am forgiven, I am clean, I am free, and I am Yours.
In Jesus' mighty Name, amen.

Welcome to the family of God. This is the first day of the best days of your life. Now, go after God with all your heart—He's got a great plan for you!

It's important to tell someone about your decision, and you'll find no one more friendly and excited about your decision than one of our great people at Revival Today. We want to hear from you. Give us a call:

412-787-2578

JONATHAN AND ADALIS SHUTTLESWORTH

Evangelists Jonathan and Adalis Shuttlesworth have been preaching the Gospel full-time since May 2002. Revival Today, founded in 2007, is a ministry dedicated to reaching those who have never heard the Gospel of Jesus Christ. Over the past 20 years, Jonathan has traveled extensively throughout North America, India, the Caribbean, and Central and South Africa. In 2013, Revival Today TV was launched on mainstream television. In recent years, Revival Today's online presence has expanded significantly through platforms like Facebook and YouTube.

Since 2015, Evangelist Jonathan has conducted numerous open-air crusades and outreaches in America's inner cities, dedicated to winning the lost. Revival Today's heartbeat is for souls. The nations of the world are overripe for revival, and we are determined to be a great part of it! Revival Today provides Biblical teaching on faith, healing, prosperity, freedom from sin, and living a victorious life.

Amidst the coronavirus pandemic in 2020, Check the News—a daily program covering breaking news through the lens of Biblical truth—was launched. That same year, the Revival Today app, a 24-hour streaming platform with on-demand content, also went live.

In early 2021, Evangelists Jonathan and Adalis made a historic announcement: the launch of Revival Today Church in Pittsburgh, Pennsylvania—a church that honors the Holy Spirit, wins souls, boldly proclaims the Word of God without apology, and stands as a blessing to families and the nation. Revival Today Church sparked a movement. Soon after, Revival Today Church Fort Worth opened its doors in October 2023, igniting a fire that would soon spread across America. In March 2025, Revival Today Church Los Angeles launched, followed just weeks later by Revival Today Church Arizona on Easter Sunday 2025. Today, with all four locations thriving, growing, and impacting their cities, the vision is alive, and the mandate is being fulfilled: to see this generation shaken by the power of God.

Pastors Jonathan and Adalis believe that anyone who feels the call of God to preach the Gospel must have a solid biblical foundation. It's a non-negotiable—but it is not enough. Strong Biblical training, combined with the power of the Holy Ghost, is essential for raising up the next generation of the world.

God has called Revival Today to establish Revival Today Bible Institute—a training school designed to equip this generation to answer His call. The mission of RTBI is clear: to raise up ministers of excellence who will deliver the Gospel of Jesus Christ with both Word and Power.

If you need help or would like to partner with Revival Today to see this generation and nation transformed through The Gospel, follow these links…

www.RevivalToday.com
www.RevivalTodayChurch.com

Get access to our 24/7 network Revival Today Global Broadcast. Download the Revival Today app in your Apple App Store or Google Play Store. Watch live on Apple TV, Roku, Amazon Fire TV, and Android TV.

Call: 412-787-2578

facebook.com/revivaltoday
x.com/jdshuttlesworth
instagram.com/jdshuttlesworth
youtube.com/@jonathanshuttlesworth

DO SOMETHING TODAY THAT WILL CHANGE YOUR LIFE FOREVER

THUS SAITH THE LORD, **MAKE THIS VALLEY FULL OF DITCHES**. FOR THUS SAITH THE LORD, YE SHALL NOT SEE WIND, NEITHER SHALL YE SEE RAIN; YET THAT VALLEY SHALL BE FILLED WITH WATER... **THIS IS BUT A LIGHT THING IN THE SIGHT OF THE LORD**... AND IT CAME TO PASS... **THE COUNTRY WAS FILLED WITH WATER.**

2 KINGS 3:16-18; 20

Revival is the only answer to the problems of this country - nothing more, nothing less, nothing else.

Thank you for standing with me as a partner with Revival Today. We must see this nation shaken by the power of God.

You cannot ask God to bless you first, prior to giving. God asks you to step out first in your giving - and then He makes it rain. We are believing God for 1,000 people to partner with us monthly at $84. Something everyone can do, but a significant seed that will connect you to the rainmaker.

IF YOU HAVE NOT YET PARTNERED WITH REVIVAL TODAY, JOIN US TODAY!

This year is not your year to dig small ditches. When I grew tired of small meetings and altar calls, I moved forward in faith and God responded. God is the rainmaker, but you must give Him something to fill. It's time for you to move forward! **Will you stand with me today to see the nations of the world shaken by the power of God?**

Revivaltoday.com/give

revivaltoday.com/paypal

Zelle® info@revivaltoday.com

 @RTgive

Text "GIVE" to 75767
Call at (412) 787-2578

Mail a check to:

Revival Today P.O. BOX 7
PROSPERITY PA 15329

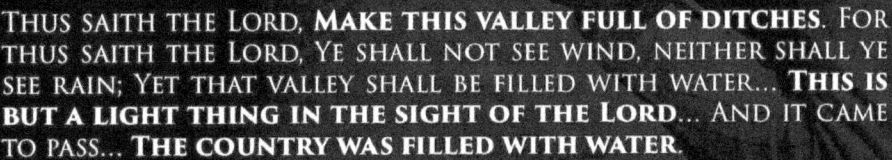

REVIVAL TODAY Email: info@revivaltoday.com

www.ingramcontent.com/pod-product-compliance
Lightning Source LLC
Chambersburg PA
CBHW050033090426
42735CB00022B/3469